UNIVERSITY COLLEGE CORK

A PORTRAIT IN WORDS AND IMAGES

Text by John A. Murphy

Images by Andrew Bradley

Coláiste na hOllscoile Corcaigh, Éire
University College Cork, Ireland

Acknowledgements

*To all those whose participation made this book possible, your help and support
is acknowledged and very much appreciated.*

First published in 2005 by the
Office of Marketing and Communications,
University College Cork,
Ireland

Edited by Nancy Hawkes and Ruth McDonnell

© Office of Marketing and Communications, UCC

All rights are reserved. No part of this book may be reprinted or reproduced or utilised
in any electronic, mechanical or other means, now known or hereafter invented,
including photocopying, without the prior written permission of
the Office of Marketing and Communications, UCC.

Images of the Honan Chapel are reproduced by kind permission of the Honan Trust.

A CIP catalogue record for this book is available from the British Library.

ISBN: 0 9502440 3 1

Designed and Typeset by Anú Design, Collierstown, Tara, Co. Meath, Ireland

Printed by Edelvives, Spain.

Contents

Foreword

This new collection of photographs makes a familiar and beloved campus appear new and exciting. I would like to think that their stimulating impact is suitably reflected in the captions and in this foreword.

The camera rightly lingers on several features of the original limestone building. The architect, Sir Thomas Deane, successfully urged the Board of Works in 1846 to choose the Gillabbey site in preference to others for the 'beauties and advantages' of its 'excellent and commanding' situation. He was excited by the dramatic idea of grouping the Aula Maxima, library and tower close to the cliff edge overlooking the river and the Western Road. The visual impact is as striking today as it was in 1849.

In the same year, the completed Main Quadrangle drew the highest praise from *The Cork Examiner*: the 'splendid structure' was a credit 'to the artistic genius and mechanical skill of our city'. Bradley's photography also highlights the stone-carved Quadrangle ornaments which were executed under the supervision of Benjamin Woodward, Deane's associate, who was strongly influenced by the stonework at Holy Cross, Co. Tipperary.

Moving out from the Quadrangle, the camera pans over the various buildings which have developed during the decades in response to the requirements of an ever-growing student body. The key to the physical character of UCC is its gradual expansion from the original core. There was never a movement to a new greenfield site. In 1994–1995, an intense and passionate debate took place on a proposal to develop the vacated Our Lady's Hospital, a mile to the northwest, as a second campus but eventually the idea receded like a mirage. There have been some extramural acquisitions to the east – academics intermittently hanker after a cityward thrust – but essentially the story is one of response to challenges of development in the vicinity of the original location. Successive expansions have not affected a certain compact unity.

The main growth of the campus has been, of necessity, westward. Beginning with the integration of the County Gaol premises from the 1950s, sites were acquired and buildings constructed over the next half-century across the Gaol Walk and right up to the Bon Secours Hospital boundary and, more recently, beyond to the Brookfield complex. East of the Quadrangle, existing structures were demolished, sometimes controversially, to provide, at the turn of the twenty-first century, a new arc of buildings and the spacious Honan Square.

Two points may be emphasised about the physical development of the campus. First, though one or two of the earlier additional buildings were pedestrian (Electrical Engineering) or downright ugly (the massive Science Building), the later ones were artistic and in harmony with the Main Quadrangle. (All, of course, provided badly needed space for students and staff.) Second, one can only applaud the ingenuity of college planners and engineers who found building space in the campus block where none apparently existed: the Boole complex and the Castlewhite apartments come to mind. Meanwhile, preservation and progress go hand in hand. On the eastern side of the campus, the Hiberno-Romanesque glory of the Honan Chapel (1916) is only two minutes' walk away from the visionary Glucksman Gallery (2004).

All of this is strikingly captured in Bradley's photographs. But they take on an even more vivid character when dealing with the human dimension. Students are shown here at study, in research labs, making music, at sport, relaxing in the leafy surrounds of the President's Garden, or celebrating their graduation. Amazingly, the extended campus

seems to have room for all of them. In the 1970s, President M.D. McCarthy expressed the view that the student body should not exceed 7,000 if the essential character of UCC was to be preserved. With the numbers now in excess of double that figure, one can only adapt Parnell's famous maxim and say that no man should set a boundary to the march of a university!

Whatever about numbers, the progressive McCarthy would have been pleased with the multicultural diversity of the student body in the early twenty-first century. The traditional provincial intake has been greatly diversified by the presence of over 2,000 students from Europe, the United States, the Middle East, India and the Far East. Obviously, this phenomenon benefits college finances and the local economy but it also adds a welcome cosmopolitan, even exotic, flavour to student life. This dimension is also reflected in Bradley's camerawork.

Perusers of these beautiful photographs may well wonder if UCC is bathed in perpetual sunshine. Good weather naturally brings out the best in buildings and humans, so we can understand why the photographer has consistently sought a brilliant sunlit context. I will add a benign conceit of my own: sunshine symbolises the eternal student who projects from age to age the charming illusion of unchanging youth. Students are always the shining hour. *Semper sint in sole.*

John A. Murphy, 2005

The Grand View

Sir Thomas Deane, the architect of Queen's College Cork, was well aware that the spectacular grouping of the tower, the library and the Aula Maxima on the cliff-edge site would have a dramatic visual impact on the spectator on the Western Road below.

This was the stunning prospect that greeted Queen Victoria as she was driven along the Western Road in August 1849. It was this 'best view' of the college that the professors, in a petition in 1874, were anxious to preserve by ensuring that it would not be obscured by the building of a continuous terrace of houses along the Western Road. Thankfully, the 'chief public view' remains unobstructed today. Discreet and subtle floodlighting adds a special nocturnal charm to the old limestone.

Macaulay's reference to 'a Gothic college worthy to stand in the High Street of Oxford' used to appear *ad nauseam* in guides to, and notices of, the college. The reverential repetition of this patronising observation smacks of colonial cringe. It should be sufficient to note that the UCC edifice is worthy to stand imposingly over the elegant western approaches to the city of Cork.

The Main Quadrangle

A three-sided quadrangle? A Cork architect's joke? Not completed for reasons of economy? Original plan scaled down when it was realised that opposition to the 'godless colleges' would mean fewer students than expected?

The only explanation deserving serious mention is that in the mid-nineteenth century enclosed quadrangles were considered to be unhealthy, stale air being thought to spread disease. But the most likely reason is that the architect, Sir Thomas Deane, simply made a deliberate design choice of an unfinished symphony, feeling, like Schubert, that it was neither necessary nor desirable to compose a closing movement. A low wall intended for the fourth side was never built. And so the light was allowed to flow in from the south, making the Main Quadrangle a place of soft brightness and tranquillity and, in (rare) sunshine, of basking warmth.

The Deane architectural firm (which included a younger brother, Kearns Deane, and Benjamin Woodward) had designed the Cork Savings Bank and St Mary's Church in classical style, but Gothic – the college style has been variously described as Perpendicular Gothic, Tudor Gothic and Victorian Gothic – had also come into fashion and was particularly acceptable for colleges, following the Oxford and Cambridge models. Deane's design most closely resembled Magdalen College, Oxford. The tower clock, manufactured by the celebrated clockmakers and jewellers, Mangans of Cork, was installed in 1851.

The building contractor was John Butler of Dublin. Construction was begun early in 1847 and finished within two years. Since the Queen's Colleges were to be non-residential and non-denominational, there was no provision for sleeping accommodation, dining halls or chapels. On the other hand, the whole east range or wing of Queen's College Cork was given over to the President's and Vice-President's houses, with a private garden behind. The north and west ranges had cloisters and offices on the ground floor while the first floor accommodated lecture rooms and laboratories in the west range, and two museums in the north range. Behind the Quadrangle, on the northeastern side, stood the library and the Aula Maxima.

The manpower involved in the construction was considerable and at least some of the workers must have been drawn from the Co. Cork countryside, who thus found some work relief from the devastating consequences of the Great Famine in the wretched years of the late 1840s.

The Clock Tower and Arch

The Clock Tower is the dominant feature of the Main Quadrangle. Originally there were tower gates in place here. Notable is the solid masonry of the vault over the archway, reputedly the first such stone vault constructed in Ireland since medieval times. The visitor walking under the archway ('the Arch') from the north suddenly comes on the quadrangle. The Arch has long been a convenient, if windy, rendezvous point. Up to the 1960s or so, the wheezy ringing of a bell in the tower would signal the ending of the lecture hour.

The Green Man

A striking feature of the quadrangle walls
is the ornamental stone carving at various
points. The decorative work includes abstract
figures and flowers, as well as bird, animal
and human images. The man's head surrounded
by foliage over the central doorway of the
North Wing may well be 'the Green Man',
a well-known decorative motif stretching
back nearly two millennia. Carved in stone or
wood or any surface open to ornamentation,
or depicted on stained glass and illuminated
manuscripts, the Green Man was a common
medieval image and featured again in the
Victorian Gothic Revival. His significance
is elusive (a wild man of the woods?), but
comparisons have been made with, among
others, Robin Hood, Jack-in-the-Green
and Baphomet.

The Door of Judgement

This interesting light-and-shade photograph silhouettes a student through the central door of the North Wing while the sun streams in through the lattice window on to a cup-and-circle stone of great antiquity from Mothel, Co. Waterford. In less humane days, the superintendent of examinations would stand on the doorstep here before apprehensive students and would brutally announce the results just decided by the examination boards. 'John A. Murphy' – honours, pass or REJECT!

Queen Victoria

During Queen Victoria's brief visit (there was cholera in the city) to Cork in August 1849, as the royal carriage passed along the Western Road, 'a statue of her Majesty, presented to the College authorities by Sir Thomas Deane [the architect] was suddenly erected to the apex of the most conspicuous gable' of the recently constructed Queen's College, according to *The Cork Examiner*, 3 August 1849. A contemporary *Illustrated London News* depicts the scene. The statue was inspired by a similar one at Lincoln's Inn. There is a nationalist tradition that disaffected workmen allowed the statue to dangle momentarily with a rope around its neck.

The limestone statue (variously attributed to Edward Ambrose or Paddy Scannell, both Cork sculptors) represents a youthful thirty-year-old Victoria in simple and pleasing medieval garb, to accord with the building's Gothic style. She is still decades away from the ample widow-figure with which we are more familiar.

In the highly charged nationalist/Catholic atmosphere of the 1930s, the college authorities dethroned Victoria from her perch atop the eastern pinnacle of the Aula Maxima and replaced her with St Finbarr, designed by the young sculptor Seamus Murphy. The Victoria statue was stored in an East Wing office for some years until its three-quarter-ton weight proved too much for the floorboards. In 1946, it was lowered into a straw-lined pit in the President's Garden and there buried by college gardeners with mock-reverent obsequies. In its semi-secret location, it was protected both from the ravages of iconoclastic nationalists and of atmospheric pollution.

As the celebration of the 150th anniversary of the college's foundation approached, the statue was dug up and cleaned by the stone conservator John Kelly. It was displayed in its present Graduates' Room location, in connection with the UCC 150 Universitas exhibition. Though there were protests in Irish and Irish-American circles at the resurrection of the 'Famine Queen', there is wide public interest in this significant reminder of the college's chequered history. And it has to be said that Victoria looks little the worse for wear after her long years of banishment and entombment!

The Royal Crest Defaced

The turbulent politics of the 1930s were reflected in Blueshirt, and more formidably in republican, activity among students. Between 2 a.m. and 4 a.m. on 31 January 1939, armed men broke into the night porter's room near the Arch, marched him to an adjacent boiler room and there bound and gagged him. They then placed a ladder against the northern wall of the tower and one of their number defaced the royal crest, smashing a large part of the crown and chipping the nose off the unicorn. The culprits remained undetected. *The Irish Times* condemned the defacement as the 'infantile' counterpart of IRA explosives at London Tube stations. 'What offence had the "inanimate unicorn" given?' asked the newspaper rhetorically. This stern lecturing from the pro-British organ must have caused self-satisfied guffaws among the perpetrators.

The students' council in UCC half-heartedly condemned the mutilation of college property but said crests on the premises should have 'an Irish or religious significance'. Registrar Alfred O'Rahilly lambasted the 'petty vandalism' of 'our young generalissimos', 'bumptious self-opinionated anarchists' and sarcastically wondered would they next start 'defacing the numerous small symbols of Lancaster and York in the College stonework'. There was a lively exchange of letters in *The Cork Examiner* between O'Rahilly and student supporters of the culprits who claimed that a National University of Ireland college should have a 'National' appearance. To the registrar's argument that there were peaceful ways of effecting nationalist action, as with the removal five years previously of the Victoria statue, the students retorted that 'the dear old lady is still tucked away intact'.

Though there was no repeat performance, the episode rankled with O'Rahilly and strengthened that authoritarian strain which was to be so evident in his presidency (1943–1954).

The Patron Saint

The replacement of the Queen Victoria statue in 1934 by that of St Finbarr should be seen in the strongly nationalist and religious context of the time. In one professor's reminiscences, what really led to Victoria's removal was the fear of the college authorities that 'republican' students would blow her up unless she was taken down. Be that as it may, it was generally felt that an 'alien' symbol should be replaced by the image of a saint whose monastic school thirteen centuries before was believed to have stood on a nearby site. 'Where Finbarr taught, let Munster learn' had long been the college motto. The strong tradition of continuity was reflected in a passage of President Robert Kane's speech on the opening day in 1849: 'Fin Barra, the patron saint of Cork . . . left to his followers the charge of founding a seat of learning in this place: here, after nearly a thousand years, we open now the portals of this edifice and accept the task of training the youth of Munster.'

The St Finbarr statue was the work of Seamus Murphy, a welcome commission for the young sculptor just back from his studies in Paris. A college society, the Academy of St Thomas, directed by the influential registrar, Alfred O'Rahilly, raised funds for the statue which was then presented to the Governing Body. It was the first such religious emblem to be accepted by a National University of Ireland college. Standing seven feet high and weighing one and a half tons, it is carved in limestone to harmonise with the prevailing architectural tone. Interestingly, Murphy depicts the saint austerely as a cowled monk with his right hand raised in blessing, rather than the conventional (and chronologically dubious) episcopal figure. A contemporary newspaper report noted that the lines of the hair and beard appeared white in the light. It should also be said that binoculars are required to view the statue clearly so that, regrettably, it is noted by very few. Here, and on the cover, Andrew Bradley gives us a soaring, celestial perspective.

Ironically, a UCC scholar's research has undermined the reality of a historical St Finbarr and, even more shockingly, has suggested that he was not a Corkman and never set foot in the place! This iconoclasm

caused quite a stir and led to a tongue-in-cheek
proposal that the motto should be changed to
'where Munster thought that Finbarr taught'.
Other facetious variants over the years have been
'where Finbarr taught, let Munster churn' (Dairy
Science activities) and '. . . let Munster earn'
(money-generating research).

Pushing their Luck?

Certain traditions are passed through successive student generations, rather like the mysterious transmission of children's street games. Thus, there was a venerable belief that those who had not 'their courses revised once' by the time (generally around St Patrick's Day) the lawnmowers appeared in the quad were doomed to examinations failure. This was an understandable counsel of prudence but the notion that walking on the central quadrangle pathways similarly presaged disaster belonged firmly to the category of superstition. The casual strollers shown below are either not students or have a rationalist disregard for such taboos – or passed their examinations long since!

The Cup and Mace

Displayed on a table in the Graduates' Room (the Staff Common Room can be glimpsed through the doorway) are a solid silver cup and the college mace. The photograph also shows the Queen Victoria statue, encased in terrorist-proof glass! The inscription on the handsome cup tells us that it was presented in 1933 to Professor Alfred O'Rahilly by the 'Cork Junior Tramwaymen' as a (presumably quite expensive) token of their appreciation. O'Rahilly was the dominant – and dominating – UCC figure of the period, as registrar from 1920 to 1943 and president from 1943 to 1954. He had a reputation for being an effective intermediary in industrial disputes and on this occasion he had helped to secure compensation for the aggrieved tramwaymen, when the Cork tram service closed down.

As the symbol of authority, the mace is displayed at Governing Body meetings and borne in academic procession at graduation ceremonies. (In the past, it also featured in the obsequies of college presidents). This fine silver and enamel mace, embellished with Celtic ornamental motifs, was commissioned in 1910 by Sir Bertram Windle, then president of the college, to mark the transition from the old Queen's College to the new University College Cork. The cost was met by subscription from staff and friends. Both cup and mace were made by the leading Cork silversmiths, William Egan and Sons. The mace was the first important order issued in Cork since the old school of silversmiths died out nearly a century before.

The Symbolic Heart

The Aula Maxima (literally 'greatest hall') was the largest single element in Deane and Woodward's design for Queen's College Cork. The Board of Works schedule had called for 'a Great Hall for public purposes, distributing prizes, opening sessions, etc.' and, from the beginning, it was also described as the Examinations Hall. The general model was the late medieval banqueting hall, but the main specific prototype appears to have been the New Hall and Library at Lincoln's Inn, opened in 1845.

In addition to its original specific uses, the Aula has served a great many other purposes down the years. It has been a study hall, a supplementary library (from 1864), a place for presidential inaugurations and graduation ceremonies, a concert and recital hall, a conference centre, a banqueting room and (at a time when no other suitable location on campus was available) a venue for college 'hops'. This writer can recall some far-from-fancy footwork on the knobbly pine floorboards which, fortunately, were not a major deterrent to the blossoming of romance!

In 2000–2002, UCC undertook a major refurbishment of the Aula, costing nearly €2 million. Every feature – roof, ceiling, floor, walls, fireplaces, pendant light fittings, gallery, bookcases – was painstakingly restored and conserved, in fidelity to the original construction methods and materials. Thus, this central symbol of continuity had its integrity guaranteed for another 150 years.

Particular attention was devoted to the two impressive stained glass windows. The window on the north wall, 'the Professor's Window', is dedicated to the memory of Robert Harkness, a Lancashire man and Professor of Mineralogy and Geology (1853–1878), who had a distinguished career as a geologist. The dominating feature of the east end of the Aula is the splendid memorial window (1866) to the great mathematician, George Boole, first Professor of Mathematics at the college. It is believed to have been inspired by Pugin's design for House of Commons windows. The lower central panel shows Boole seated, writing, with Aristotle (left) and Euclid (right) behind him.

The Symbolic Heart continued . . .

On the west wall, hang the portraits of the successive presidents of the college, from Sir Robert Kane (1849–1873) onwards. Because of the importance of the office of president, the portraits comprise a compendium of college history, or at least a significant feature of it. Sometimes facetiously referred to as a 'rogues' gallery, the display in fact includes only two rogues. The rest range from the mediocre to the outstanding – not forgetting the vain: one colourful president complained to the portraitist that he had made the previous (inadequate) incumbent appear as intelligent as himself!

The Aula Maxima has been the object of superlatives from the beginning down to the present. *The Cork Examiner* described it as 'one of the most magnificent rooms in Ireland' in September 1849. Two months afterwards, in describing the colourful opening ceremonies on 7 November 1849, the same paper remarked that the 'magnificent' Aula, with its great hammerbeam trusses, already looked mellow, although only just completed. Though now too small for some conferring ceremonies, the Aula remains the iconic centre of UCC, the ceremonial and symbolic heart of the college.

The Ogham Stones and Stone Corridor

There are 28 Ogham (or Ogam) stones in the cloister walk, or Stone Corridor, in the North and West Wings of the quadrangle. They constitute the largest collection of Ogham stones on public display in Ireland. They were variously acquired by the college from the mid-nineteenth to the early twentieth century. (The Stone Corridor is also home to some non-Ogham items – a rotary quern, two cup-and-circle stones and a cross-inscribed memorial.)

The invention of the Ogham style of alphabet writing has been attributed to Ogma mac Elethan of the Tuatha Dé Danann. The inscriptions are the earliest written source of the Irish language and the oldest documentation of Irish personal names. This peculiar monument-script flourished between the mid-fifth and the late seventh centuries. It consists of a series of twenty characters arranged in four groups, each group made up of one to five scores, cut to the right or left or diagonally across a stemline, generally the edge of the stone. The inscription records the name of the man (in only one case a woman, on a Welsh stone) being commemorated, and it tells us whose son or descendant or devotee he was.

There are about 330 stones in Ireland, with a large concentration (260) in south Munster, over a hundred being in Co. Kerry. Forty Ogham inscriptions have been found in Wales, seven in Devon and Cornwall and five in the Isle of Man – all reflecting the Irish diaspora of the period. All Ogham inscriptions are in Irish, but the British ones are bilingual, having Latin equivalents. While some inscriptions are clearly legible, others are difficult to decipher, the lettering having suffered from the secondary uses to which many of the stones were put – as building material in early and medieval constructions, and subsequently in gateways and outhouses – before they were rediscovered and rescued.

The removal of the stones from their sites by antiquarians would hardly be condoned today and even a century ago was denounced in some quarters as vandalism, particularly in a case where President Bertram Windle was the culprit! But scholars have benefited from ready access to the collection which is now the subject of a UCC policy of conservation, reorganisation and display. It may also be noted that familiarity over the decades with stones on open display has not, happily, resulted in any major defacement or damage by students!

Coffee Break – the Staff Common Room

From the foundation of Queen's College Cork in 1849, the library was housed in the north range behind the quadrangle in a space of double-storey height. Later, an intermediate floor was constructed and, after the opening of the Boole Library in 1983, the ground floor of the old library became the new Common Room, with the floor above accommodating various council meetings. Note the rather low ceiling of the room and, in the top left-hand corner, the elaborate chimney-piece (in the original library) with carvings inspired by the panels of the Waking Bier at Holy Cross Abbey, Co. Tipperary.

It has been observed that the Common Room has the homely and comfortable ambience of a second-class lounge in an ocean liner. More seriously, the room lives up to its egalitarian title: membership is open to staff of all ranks, grades, ages and genders.

Mr Dudley O'Driscoll

The College Community

The phrase 'college community' suggests that a university comprises academic staff and students only. In reality, UCC is less one family than a series of families occupying the same space. Academics, students, administrators, librarians, technicians and security/services personnel – all subconsciously feel the college is *their* particular territorial realm. Certainly, the place could not function without the infrastructure of services and security. Those who dwell far from the upper reaches of a charmed academic circle are often animated by a strong sense of collegiality and by affection for, and loyalty to, a hallowed institution.

Otium cum Dignitate

The hallowed phrase *otium cum dignitate*
can be colloquially, and very freely, translated
as 'taking it easy in honourable and adequately
pensioned retirement'. But, despite appearances
here, it would be inappropriate to apply the
description to Dr Tomás Ó Canainn, the
doyen of Irish traditional musicians, popular
Derryman long located in Cork and former
UCC lecturer in such diverse disciplines as
electrical engineering and music. He barely
has time to scan this newspaper, being still
vigorously and bilingually (sometimes
multilingually) active in his *uomo universale*
pursuits as piper, composer, singer, poet,
novelist and lecturer.

Dr Tomás Ó Canainn

'Then felt I like some watcher of the skies'

The Crawford Observatory was named after W.H. Crawford, a wealthy brewer, a friend and admirer of W.K. Sullivan (President, 1873–1890) and one of the very few substantial benefactors in the history of the college. He was a generous donor to the library and was a leading sponsor of the observatory, built in 1880, which bears his name. He put up funds to enable the college to join a celestial photography and mapping programme to be undertaken from the observatory and he provided a substantial sum towards the purchase of astronomical instruments. But there were other sponsors as well, notably the very interested eighth Duke of Devonshire.

The limestone observatory has Gothic architectural features in harmony with the main college buildings. It was in full working order by the mid-1880s. It reflected the intense contemporary public interest in astronomy and meteorology. Howard Grubb of Dublin built the observatory and its fittings, including the revolving telescope dome, clocks and astronomical instruments. The most important of these was an 8.5 inch telescope, equatorially mounted, which was exhibited at the Paris Exhibition in 1878 where it was awarded a gold medal.

Though the citizens at large enjoyed indulging their bent as amateur astronomers when visiting the observatory (this writer recalls viewing the splendid spectacle of Jupiter and its moons in the 1960s), its intramural importance gradually declined and it had only a marginal place in courses of study. The virtually unimpeded celestial view commanded by the main telescope was gradually restricted by successive new buildings. The observatory itself fell into some disrepair and part of it was used as a music room in the 1930s!

Nevertheless, the Physics Department always maintained a research interest there and from the late twentieth century its significance in architectural terms and in the history of Irish scientific technology has been widely appreciated. An exciting restoration project is now in train, made possible by generous private funding. General interest in astronomy will be renewed by the observatory's return to full working order with the restored original instruments and by its use as a teaching facility for the astrophysics degree programme. It will also be an interpretative centre for the history of Irish astronomy. Finally, visits from the public and from school children will once again fulfil the observatory's original objective and this will be a fitting tribute to the vision of Sullivan, Crawford and Grubb.

The Boole Library

This new library, opened in September 1983, was a necessary response to the rapid expansion of student numbers in the 1960s and 1970s. It was built on the site of the old quarry (between the quadrangle and College Road) from which limestone had been excavated to construct the original college buildings.

Nostalgic graduates regretted the new development, recalling the muddily titanic inter-faculty sporting battles in the Quarry in their golden student days while conveniently forgetting the hazards of a thin and stony pitch surface and the inconvenient noise levels for neighbouring lecture halls. The splendid five-storey structure, as well as its underground complex of lecture halls and offices, was named after George Boole, the great mathematician and the most renowned professor (1849–1864) in the history of the institution. An autodidact from Lincoln, he is best remembered for his development of Boolean algebra which underlies computer science. He died, aged 49, in December 1864, having caught pneumonia after walking four miles in a rainstorm from his Ballintemple home to his lectures.

The Boole Library again exemplified the already proven ingenuity of college planners in resourcefully finding new locations in a small campus area. Moreover, the new building gracefully completed the unfinished symphony of the quadrangle, with the ancient trees on the embankment acting effectively as an aesthetically pleasing screen.

Loyal Waterford

On the old College Road entrance, the pedestrian or wicket gate displays, among other crests, the Waterford City coat of arms with its motto *Urbs Intacta Manet* ('the city remains untaken'). Unlike rebel Cork, Waterford rejected the Yorkist Pretender, Perkin Warbeck in 1495, successfully resisting an eleven-day siege. Henry VII recognised this loyalty to the Tudors (to be demonstrated again during the rising of Silken Thomas in the 1530s) by awarding the city its famous motto.

Waterford has also been loyal to UCC, consistently sending the college the cream of its students over the decades.

The O'Rahilly Building

The O'Rahilly Building (1997) and the
Devere Hall/Áras na Mac Léinn (1995),
together with the Honan Chapel (1916) in
between, embrace an attractive new plaza
at the eastern end of the campus, backing on
to Donovan's Road. The extensive O'Rahilly
Building stands on the southeastern corner
of the campus block, where the men's
residential Honan Hostel used to be. It is a
splendid architectural composition, all glittering
blocks of limestone and glass. It provides
staff offices and lecture/seminar rooms for
a wide range of disciplines in the humanities,
social sciences and business.

It is UCC policy to commemorate, where
possible, significant figures from the college's
past, by naming (or renaming) buildings in
their honour. (Of course, hard financial realities
dictate that present-day benefactors, often
unconnected with UCC, must also be included
in the naming process.) This building fittingly
recalls the dynamic and controversial Alfred
O'Rahilly, the dominant UCC figure
of the first half of the twentieth century
(Registrar 1920–1943, President 1943–1954).

Apart from his central role as a vibrant and
effective president, the wide range of his
scholarly interests – politics, sociology, finance,
Christology, mathematical physics, history –
makes O'Rahilly an appropriate choice for
commemoration in a structure which serves
multi-disciplinary purposes. His remarkable
career is summarised in an impressive tablet
in the central hall of the building.

BioSciences Institute

Here is an extensive ultra-modern building, constructed in the early years of the third millennium, and dedicated to multi-disciplinary research in the biomedical sciences. To add to the modern image, the institute is located at the western limits of the campus, representing yet another ambitious stage in UCC's western expansion, a process begun in the late 1940s with the acquisition of the County Gaol premises.

Teamwork, sharing funding and equipment, and collaboration with industry are the hall-marks of the institute. Its researchers have international experience and contacts. They also benefit from a new and serious commit-ment by the State to research. A turning point here was the setting up of the Science Foundation of Ireland as a funding arm of the government, a spur to scientific endeavour and a recognition that leading-edge research in the universities was indispensable to the development of the knowledge economy. Scientists might still grumble that funding is inadequate but at least politicians no longer twitter patronisingly about researchers' 'pet projects'!

The Tyndall National Institute

In recent years, the National Microelectronics Research Centre (NMRC) has been the aspect of UCC most associated in the public mind with scientific research successfully applied to 'high-tech' business. Operating as a quasi-independent sector, the NMRC has been housed in a scenic riverside location at the Lee Maltings, a converted brewery malting house ten minutes walk from the main campus. In 1996 a new office wing was built connected by an atrium with the historic 'Maltings'

A further major development took place in July 2004 when the government made substantial state funding available to upgrade the Lee Maltings complex and established the Tyndall National Institute (TNI) comprising the NMRC, the Photonics Research communities within UCC and the Cork Institute of Technology (CIT), and relevant physics activities within UCC. The TNI makes its extensive research facilities widely available; forms partnerships with researchers in relevant fields; and establishes joint R&D programmes with industry. While operating as a functioning part of the university system with a pronounced teaching role, the TNI is not alone by far the largest institute of its kind in Ireland but aspires to be one of the major ICT research centres in Europe.

And who was the eponymous Tyndall? John Tyndall (1820–1893), a native of Leighlinbridge,

Co Carlow, was one of Ireland's most noted scientists. Largely self-educated, he first worked for the Ordnance Survey and, in 1853, was appointed professor of natural philosophy at the Royal Institute where he became the most famous popular lecturer of his day. In 1867 he succeeded Michael Faraday as the superintendent of the Institution.

Tyndall's many research areas included heat radiation, diamagnetism, the transmission of sound, meteorology and bacteriology. He made the first study of atmospheric pollution in London. His demonstration of the 'light-pipe' prefigured developments in modern communications technology. His inventions included a fireman's respirator, the fibre optic and the infra-red analyser. He was also a keen mountaineer and glaciologist. Towns in North America, and mountain peaks elsewhere are named after him. Perhaps he is best known for being the first person to explain why the sky is blue (Tyndall Blue) – because of the scattering of light by small particles of water.

Thus John Tyndall is a most appropriate inspirational patron of the leading Irish scientific research institute.

The researcher in the Microsystems laboratory (which provides a foundry service to the wider Tyndall fabrication) is holding a disc to camera, and unwittingly projecting an image which to the admiring layman, seems not only high-tech but positively sci-fi!

Áras na Laoi, formerly La Retraite

This building was originally Lee Cottage, situated in spacious grounds just west of the Gaol Walk, and it was the residence of the governor of the County Gaol, adjoining (and long since incorporated in) the college. It later became the home of the Murphy-O'Connor family but had fallen into disrepair when, through the good offices of Bishop Daniel Coholan of Cork, it was taken over by the La Retraite sisters, a French order specialising in hostel accommodation for ladies. It was opened as a hall of residence for women students in October 1923 and, after a new wing was built in 1967, it housed 90 students. In December 1977 it was acquired by UCC, renamed Áras na Laoi and modernised and greatly extended to accommodate various departments, lecture rooms and the audio-visual unit. Meanwhile, the La Retraite residents found a new home in nearby College Road, but this went out of business within twelve years or so.

The concept of closely supervised, boarding-school-style halls of residence belonged to an age of an authoritarian Catholic university ethos. The demise of 'Lara' and similar institutions took place when their original rationale became no longer suited to the now secularised times, giving rise to the development of self-catering apartments in the late twentieth century.

The acquisition of La Retraite by the college and its adaptation as Áras na Laoi represented another stage in the dynamic of western expansion from the original campus.

The Western Gates

When the UCC gatehouse was demolished
after the ferro-concrete bridge at the Western
Road entrance collapsed in the November
1916 flood, the splendid wrought-iron gates
(fabricated by Perrot in French Church Street
in 1879), together with their limestone archway, were salvaged. As a fine example of
Cork craftsmanship, they were exhibited in
London before being re-erected (with the
limestone archway) in their present location
shown here, at the western, or Gaol, entrance.

The Gaol Portico

The college was built next door to the County Gaol which was regarded by the academics as an unpleasant and insalubrious neighbour. However, by the 1940s, the gaol premises were in disrepair or underused, being now home to 20 or 30 borstal boys. UCC needed to expand westwards and, by agreement with the government, acquired a one-acre portion of the site fronting on College Road in the late 1940s, and the remaining 2.5 acres in 1957. The dominant Science (Kane) Building was built on this latter area in 1968–1971. The gaol had been designed in 1818 by the brothers James and George Richard Pain, and still preserved is the fine front wall with the impressive classical portico, derived from the Temple of Bacchus at Athens.

To the west of the portico are two plaques: the larger, executed by Seamus Murphy in 1947 and framed in bronze, commemorates the patriot dead of the 1919–1923 period associated with the site, while a smaller tablet was erected in 1990, unofficially and in defiance of Governing Body disapproval. It recalls the shooting dead of an IRA prisoner in 1940.

The Patriot Grave

In the mid-1940s, the Old IRA Men's Association campaigned to have a fitting monument erected over the graves of those comrades who had died on hunger strike or who were executed during the War of Independence. Their bodies had been taken from Victoria (now Collins) Barracks to the County Gaol and had been buried there in a part of the former exercise yard. The interests of the association, the college and, indeed, the government now converged: on acquiring the gaol site from the government for building expansion, the college would take over responsibility for the graves and the proposed monument, and the public could access the memorial through a new approach road from College Road.

And so it was agreed. The approach road is now the everyday traffic route into the college, running along where the gaol boundary wall used to be. Here the graves' memorial was erected and solemnly unveiled by Eamon de Valera in July 1948. The handsome monument records the names of the dead volunteers, though not all of those listed are buried here. It is carved in an ornamental, if some-what florid, style. It is well maintained and occasionally floodlit, and commemorative ceremonies take place there every Easter.

Since it was erected, generations of students have daily passed it by, as part of a taken-for-granted college landscape. Most of them are unaware that it is a patriot grave and, in a post-nationalist age, perhaps they are not interested. Yet it was the hope of the monument's planners that 'it would be a reminder to those attending Munster's seat of learning of the sacrifices made by the generation that achieved the country's freedom'.

The Honan Chapel

The Honans were a wealthy Cork merchant family whose benefactions to UCC included a prestigious undergraduate scholarship, a biological institute, a hostel for Catholic male students (formerly St Anthony's Hall) and, pre-eminently, the Honan Chapel. The Honan trust funds were mediated through Sir John R. O'Connell, a lawyer and later a priest, who, in collaboration with President Bertram Windle, was responsible for the development of the hostel and chapel.

The Honan Chapel is an exquisite example of revival Hiberno-Romanesque architecture. Modelled on such templates as Cormac's Chapel on the Rock of Cashel and St Cronan's Church at Roscrea, the chapel brilliantly reflects the best skills of the arts and crafts movement of the early twentieth century, a time of conscious Celtic revival. This is evident in so many impressive features of the interior – radiant stained-glass windows, the exotic mosaics of the tiled floor, the beautiful enamelled tabernacle and the various liturgical and rubrical furnishings. There are various published guides to the Honan Chapel but its

wonders are best reflected in the sumptuous volume, *The Honan Chapel: A Golden Vision*, edited by Virginia Teehan and Elizabeth Wincott Heckett (Cork University Press, 2004).

The opening of the Honan Chapel, dedicated to St Finbarr in 1916, signified that the new University College was at last acceptable to the Catholic bishops, though the chapel railings indicated that it was technically outside the non-denominational institution. After the Second Vatican Council, the chapel was sensitively re-ordered to meet the new liturgical requirements, without in any way deviating from the integrity of the interior. Today, the chapel ecumenically serves the needs of a pluralist student body, it lends itself to musical and choral recitals and it continues to be a popular location for graduate weddings.

For years, it was obscured by other college buildings (including the Honan Biological Building) but with their recent demolition, the beautiful limestone chapel stands splendidly revealed, harmoniously flanked by the Devere Hall/Áras na Mac Léinn and by the O'Rahilly Building.

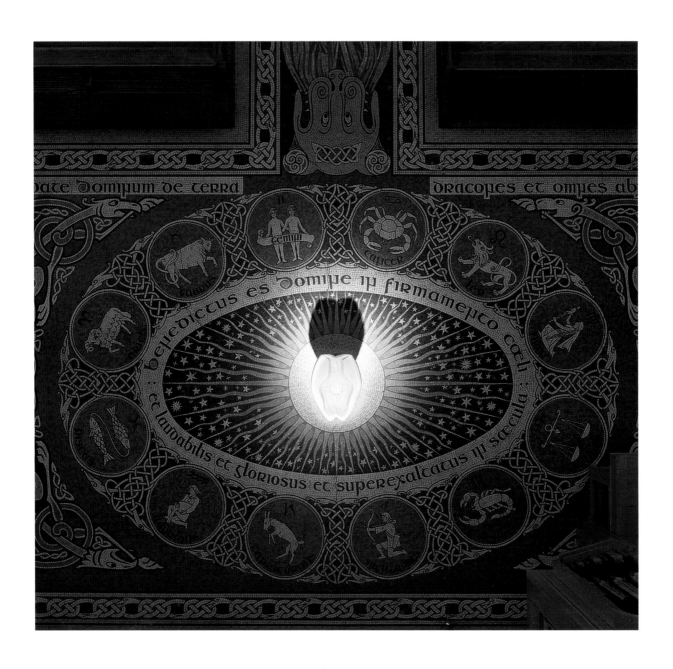

A Bird's-Eye View

A fine elevated shot from the tower, affording a bird's-eye view of part of the East Wing (with the president's office door in the centre), the President's Garden behind (obscured) and, in the background, the Honan Chapel (left) and the northern end of the O'Rahilly Building (right).

The President's Office

Through this leafy doorway, there is access not only to the president's office but to other sections of the administration in the East Wing. From the beginning of Queen's College Cork in 1849, the East Wing was a residential area, with the president living in the northern section and the vice-president occupying the remainder. When the vice-presidency lapsed in 1875, the registrar, the new second in command, became the tenant in the southern half. The rooms in the wing still have a residual domestic character, notably the fine chimney pieces. When Registrar Alfred O'Rahilly (1920–1943) became president (1943–1954), he continued to reside in the southern half while the new registrar, Henry St J. Atkins, was provided with a house on Donovan's Road. When O'Rahilly retired in 1954, virtually the whole East Wing became an administrative area.

The days of the live-in president were over, with a consequent diminution of the headmasterish supervision of students.

The President's Garden

Looking at these informal and relaxed
student groups, it is hard to believe that, in the
mid-twentieth century, a college rule sternly –
and puritanically – enjoined that 'women
students shall not lie about on the grass'. The
innocuous word 'about' somehow conveyed
an attitude of lascivious abandon.

The President's Garden was a feature of
the mildly manorial lifestyle enjoyed by earlier
college presidents. The president and vice-
president had private doorways to the walled-in
garden behind the quadrangle. During Cork's
conservative version of the student revolution
of the 1960s, one of the students' moderate
demands was that the President's Garden
should be opened up to general access.
When this was conceded, surprisingly little
use was made of it. Perhaps the demand
had been more symbolic than anything else
or perhaps pressure of study and Cork
weather were not conducive to lolling about.

Still, this verdant garden really 'is a
lovesome thing, God wot', particularly in the
spring and early summer, with its tall trees
and carefully tended shrubs and flower beds
and, for an all too brief couple of weeks in
April, its glorious cherry blossoms. Students
and staff gather here on degree day for formal
class photographs with the president. It is also
an ideal setting for photographing those
glamorous wedding groups from the nearby
Honan Chapel. And though it's not exclusively
his anymore, the president can still enjoy the
scene through his office windows!

Statuary

The introduction of nude statues to the
President's garden in the 1990s, was an
adventurous development, which no doubt
triggered sepulchral rotations among some
of the more prudish presidential predecessors.
But the statuary also serves the practical
purpose of providing back support on a
fine summer's day . . .

Neighbours

Back in 1919, President Bertram Windle found it astonishing 'how many residents of Cork had never been inside the College grounds'. He would have been similarly astonished a century later. Yet the people of the immediate neighbourhood have always been on familiar terms with the beautiful grounds – walking their dogs or relaxing in the quadrangle. These two gentlemen sharing a joke are as much at home with the modern Áras amenities as their predecessors ever were on the original campus.

Mr Donie Power and Mr Roger Ahern

A Peaceful Haven

The secluded grassy area of the Lower
Grounds, below the cliff-top, has long been
a favourite student retreat. Here one may
enjoy a leisurely stroll or cycle along the
riverside path, or read or meditate among
the trees. Romantic trysts and amorous
dalliances may be held far from prying
eyes and this privacy was particularly
appreciated in more puritanical times.
An interesting point about this charming
spot is that, although student numbers have
increased a hundredfold over a century and a
half, the amenities of the Lower Grounds
always seemed to have been experienced at
any given time by only an appreciative few.

Mr Noel O'Mahony

Landscape of UCC

When visitors comment favourably on the UCC campus, their visual impressions are formed not only by the buildings and the spatial relationships, but by the cultivated landscape, which has been under the diligent care of generations of gardeners. Carefully tended lawns and flower beds may indeed please the eye, but it is the great trees – on the avenue, in the President's Garden, on the cliff edge, on the Boole embankment and in the Lower Grounds – which are the really imposing feature of the college landscape. Mature beeches and oaks go back to the college's foundation in the late 1840s, or even earlier. Tree plantation, at a time of plentiful labour, greatly preoccupied 'improving' landlords and polite society in general, in the nineteenth century.

Rare specimens of plants collected from exotic locations were preserved in the college's botanical gardens and hothouses.

The trees on campus are affected by the forces of nature and by the exigencies of college developments. A severe storm in 1974 destroyed some of the fine specimens, and others succumbed to the ravages of Dutch elm disease in the mid-1980s. On the other hand, a major planting initiative during the college's sesquicentennial (1995) will help to transform the scene for centuries ahead. New buildings like the Lewis Glucksman Gallery and the Boole postgraduate library involved the moving or relocation of trees. Moreover, an integral feature of the marvellous Glucksman structure is the framing context of mature trees.

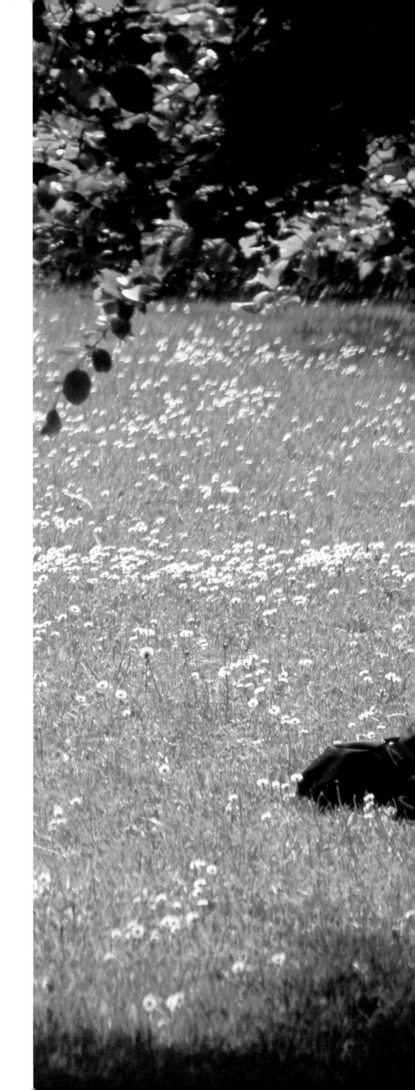

Common Oak in the Lower Grounds

The intriguing story of this tree is told by
former head gardener Harry Glavin in a
memoir in the *UCC Record* of 1967. Two
young officers from Castletownshend on
leave from the Great War (1914–1918), had
been staying with President Bertram Windle.
On their return to the front, one of them
was killed in action. Some time later, the
other officer found a tiny oak tree which had
sprouted from an acorn in his friend's tunic
pocket. The surviving officer carefully brought
it back to Cork where Glavin planted it in
memory of the slain soldier. It soon became a
memorial to both men since the survivor
also died in action shortly afterwards.

The Glucksman Gallery

When the idea of a purpose-built art gallery (and riverside restaurant) in the Lower Grounds was first mooted, some academics were apprehensive. It was felt that the tranquillity of this restful parkland area would be so compromised that its very ambience would be destroyed. In the event, such fears proved groundless. The 'footprint' of the new building was no bigger than that of the tennis court and shabby wooden pavilion which had long occupied the city end of the secluded grounds. Not alone was there no further encroachment on the existing space, but the stunning new structure enhanced the grounds and the approaches in entirely unexpected ways.

The Lewis Glucksman Gallery, costing €12 million (designed by architects O'Donnell and Twomey and opened in 2004 by the President of Ireland, Mary McAleese) is in honour of a wealthy New Yorker and his third generation Irish-American wife, Loretta Brennan Glucksman.

The materials used in the 2,000-square metre building are (once again) native limestone in the lower levels and American oak in the upper areas. From the outside, it presents the appearance of a series of limestone and glass boxes around a central axis: a great carved wooden structure, punctuated with windows, is cantilevered out from the main building and rests on slender stilts. Two large galleries give a striking sense of space and presence. The seemingly airborne structure is framed at the level of the surrounding mature trees. Overall, the Gallery strikingly manages to blend in with, as well as stand out from, its surroundings. The lower campus and the Western Road afford fine views of the building while the visitor within the gallery looks out at no less striking vistas. One hopes that it is not too smugly Corkish to observe that there is no comparable space in Ireland for contemplating works of art.

In 2005, it was given the Best Public Building award by the Royal Institute of Architects of Ireland, being described as 'a limestone pier and a timber treasure-house in the trees: dreamy and poetic, which repositions the viewer at the centre of the experience of art.'

This imaginative and stunning gallery, in itself a work of art, is as much town as gown. Situated at the most accessible point of the college to the city, it adds significantly to Cork's visual arts amenities. And it will play no small part in developing the artistic sensibilities of Cork and Munster children.

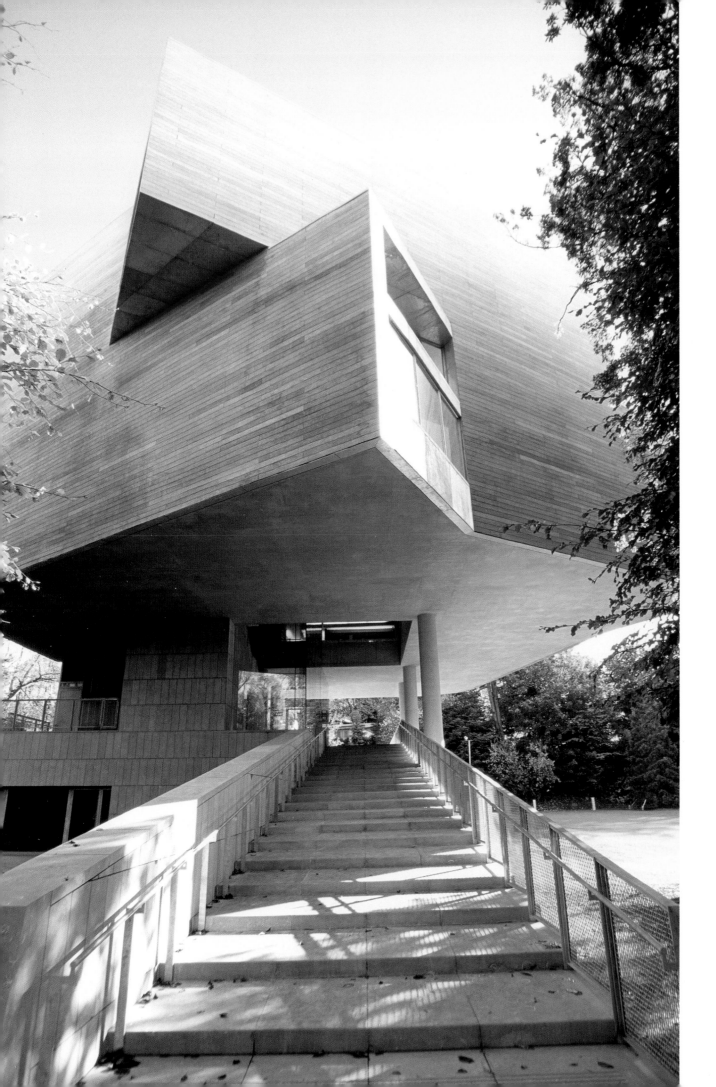

The Main Gates, Western Road

For the first 30 years (1849–1879) of its existence, the college authorities were anxious to secure a suitable entrance from the Western Road, reasonably near to town. Their concern had to do with convenience, prestige, psychology and security. The original western entrance (by the Gaol Cross) was too close to the insalubrious gaol and too far from town, with a consequent loss of public interest in the College. There was a gateway on College Road from 1864, but this did not become acceptable until the area became gentrified some time later.

In 1879 a new gate, with a wooden bridge behind, was opened at a point some yards to the west of the present main gates, shown here. A ferro-concrete structure replaced the wooden bridge in 1910 but this was swept away in severe flooding in November 1916. In any case, this entrance would have become increasingly subject to the hazards of modern traffic, not to mention the Muskerry Railway.

The task of building a worthy new entrance and bridge was long delayed, partly because of war-induced shortage of finance and materials. There was also a problem of soft foundations which necessitated deep-pile drivings in the riverbed. Finally, the impressive new entrance was completed by October 1929. It was positioned across the Donovan's Road/Western Road junction. Designed by Cork architects O'Connor and O'Flynn, it consisted of two large cut-stone pieces (later described as 'solid but graceful') with ornamental wrought-iron gates and railings, and the college coat-of-arms in an overhead arch. Behind the gates, were a new avenue and a ferro-concrete bridge in one 60-foot arch, with ornamental side-railings

like those at the entrance. The gates were executed by Messrs McLaughlin, Dublin and the railings by John Buckley and Sons, Cork.

Irish speakers were indignant that the inscription on the gates was not bilingual. Surely, said a letter writer to *The Cork Examiner*, the 'galaxy of Irish professors' should be able to frame a suitable version of the 'Where Finbarr taught' motto. In response to Gaelic League representations,

such a translation was indeed composed early in 1930 and it replaced the English original on the new gates: *Ionad Bhairre Sgoil na Mumhan.*

President Merriman had made a strong case to the government that a fine new entrance, lodge and main avenue would necessitate a correspondingly impressive building for the new dairy science institute (now the Geography Building). Certainly, the imposing new entrance opened up an uninterrupted view of the college and the grounds. *The Cork Examiner* claimed the entrance would be one of the city's principal landmarks. It was seen by some as artistically and symbolically impressive, seeming to usher in the plain citizen's yearning to be educated. Unfortunately, the gates have remained closed for many decades now. This is a matter of traffic logistics and should not be seen as a spurning of the ideal of equality of educational opportunity!

Devere Hall/Áras na Mac Léinn

The new student centre (1995) commemorates the name of an American benefactor but it was the students themselves, through a levy on their fees and grants, who enthusiastically took the financial initiative in providing this handsome Áras. It centralises many of the student services on campus, including a coffee shop, bar, photocopying services, travel office, food store, newsagent, stationery shop, meeting rooms and a radio station. The great multi-functional hall is an additional and welcome college facility, available for large-scale graduation ceremonies, banquets and big assemblies.

Situated just east of the President's Garden, its impressive glass frontage seems full of reflections, enhancing the sense of spaciousness and light. Like the matching O'Rahilly Building across the Honan Square, its many windows afford delightfully unexpected vistas of the undulating urban landscape nearby. Internally and externally, Áras na Mac Léinn is a new hub of student congregation. In far less populous days up to the end of the 1970s, when the library was still located in the North Wing, students tended to cluster socially in the Stone Corridor and in the quadrangle pathway outside. After the opening of the Boole Library in 1983, students swarmed in the area between the Main Restaurant and the Boole complex. Now the centre of gravity stretches eastward to the spacious student centre.

A Diverse Student Body

UCC has always been conscious of its perception, especially by condescending metropolitans, as smugly provincial, indeed literally so. Cork city and county, and the South Munster area, had been the almost exclusive catchment areas from the beginning, although some foreign students arrived in the post-World War II upheaval. However, the scene really began to change from the 1980s: European-sponsored schemes such as ERASMUS, as well as the Junior Year Abroad programmes with US colleges, added a marked cosmopolitan flavour to the campus. This has become more pronounced recently with an ever increasing number of arrivals from the Middle East, India and the Far East. In 2004, 75 different nationalities were represented in UCC, comprising more than 2,000 students, or about 12 per cent of the total body, and generating a welcome multi-million-euro income for the university. This phenomenon is a microcosm of the new Ireland, where historical emigration patterns have been reversed and immigrant workers are indispensable to a flourishing economy.

The Mutual Admiration of Peoples' Republics

In the early 2000s, China became an important focus of student recruitment, with the largest number of Chinese students at UCC coming from Shanghai, which is twinned with Cork and is also a second city – with all that phrase implies for mentality and attitudes.

Pictured here are members of the Chinese website team, UCC being the only university in the State with its own website in Mandarin Chinese (www.ucc.ie/chinese).

Wearing the red 'people's republic' T-shirts in front of the Quadrangle Tower, these students clearly appreciate the quirky humour of their independent-minded host city, and the cheeky cross-reference to their home country's recent history.

The Honan Square

In this striking picture, we look through the tall windows of Áras na Mac Léinn out on to the busy Honan Square and across to the O'Rahilly Building, with the Boole Library in the background (right).

Aoibhinn beatha an scoláire . . .

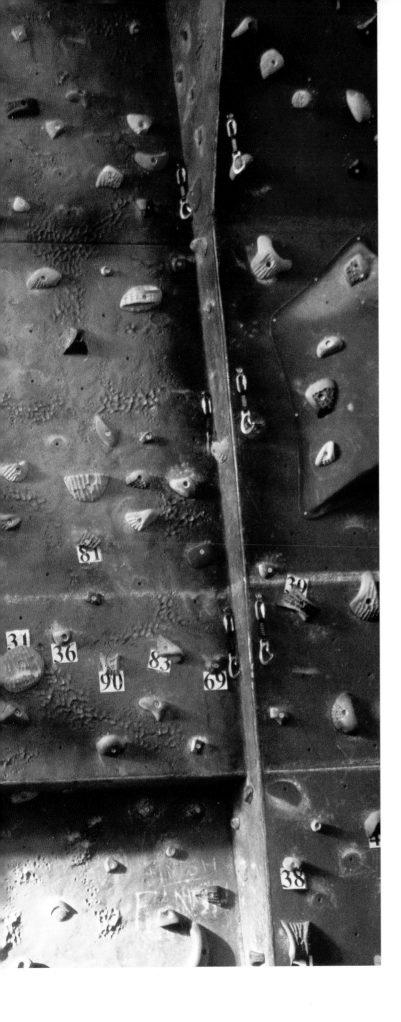

Mens sana in corpore sano . . .

When UCC acquired the Mardyke Athletic
Grounds in 1911, President Bertram Windle
confided to the Irish Chief Secretary,
Augustine Birrell, that the sports side of
college life was 'a very necessary thing with
so many ramping young men about'.
A century later, with so many thousands of
'ramping' young men – and women – about,
numerous forms of sporting activities
(including wall-climbing in the Sports Centre)
afford greatly enhanced opportunities for the
sublimation of 'ramping' proclivities.

The Snap of the Hurl

The 'clash of the ash' is a favourite nostalgic cliché of hurling reporters. It evokes heroic individual encounters in local competitions on country pitches. But 'the clash' is no longer to be heard today in the great stadia of the Gaelic Athletic Association, where it is drowned out by the roars of tens of thousands of spectators.

In this photograph of a training session at the UCC grounds in the Mardyke, the 'clash' dramatically becomes 'the snap of the ash', a not uncommon occurrence but rarely caught on camera. Note the *sliotar*, the distinctive hurling ball, in mid-picture.

In the early twentieth century, the dominant UCC field game was rugby, strongly identified with the Medical School – hence the 'skull and crossbones' logo imposed on the college colours of red and black. Gradually from the 1920s, the 'native' game flourished in the college. While GAA leaders in city and county welcomed this development, they also pointed out from time to time that the students were privileged in having more time and better facilities than were available to outside clubs whose teams were drawn from full-time workers. With UCC participating in the county championships, it was felt that the playing field was not level! Moreover, some students experienced a conflict of loyalty between college and native parish.

Over the decades, UCC has had its share of hurling and Gaelic football successes, both at county level and in inter-varsity championships (Fitzgibbon Cup in hurling, Sigerson Cup in football). However, hurling is indisputably *the* native code, immemorially rooted in Irish life, legend and literature. For purists, it is the beautiful game *par excellence*. Such aficionados are condescending about Gaelic football, which they regard as an artificial composite – if not indeed alien!

94

Mr Lacy taught her how to sing . . .

Tradition has it that the college's first lecturer in music (1903–1909), Frederick St John Lacy (Professor, 1909–1934) owed his appointment mainly to the desire of Edith Mary Windle, the wife of the then president, to avail herself of his expert services as a singing instructor, though it appears that Windle himself 'had neither taste nor liking' for music!

Irish music was a special interest of Lacy's successor, Professor Aloys Fleischmann (1936–1980) and a Cork Corporation lectureship in this subject was also established. But it was Seán Ó Riada (Lecturer, 1963–1971), the personification of the vibrant resurgence of Irish traditional music in the nation at large, who became most associated with its promotion in UCC. Micheál Ó Súilleabháin and Tomás Ó Canainn continued that tradition. The *uilleann* pipes (wind supplied by the elbowed arm, from the Irish word, *uille*, meaning 'elbow') and the harp (Irish and concert harps shown here) are celebrated and revered national instruments. In recent years, traditional music in UCC has explored the comparative dimension, broadening into ethnomusicology and experimenting with blends of the native and the exotic.

'They have their exits and their entrances . . .'

A scene from an MA Drama and Theatre
Studies production *Out of Caesar*, staged at
the Granary Theatre, UCC. In the opening
section shown here, the actors are abstractly
representing Brutus' nightmare.

In the 1980s, the student Dramatic Society
(the 'Dramat') was provided with a stage
premises in a former 'maltings' building,
which the college had acquired near the Mercy
Hospital. The Dramat's new home was in
what had been the granary section of the
malting process. The name was retained
when the theatre was relocated in 1994
to an independent building in the Mardyke
(in the Presentation complex), situated,
appropriately, half-way between the campus
and the city.

The development of the Granary has taken
place in conjunction with the growth of
Drama and Theatre Studies as undergraduate
and postgraduate programmes. More than 100
students study, work and perform in the theatre.
The work is multi-disciplinary – theatre, dance,
art and music – with a lively and critical
programme of talks, workshops and artists'
presentations.

From the outset, the emphasis has been on
the modern (the Dramat's first production was
Bertolt Brecht's *The Caucasian Chalk Circle*)
and the avant-garde. The Granary introduces
experimental works by international artists,
as well as serving UCC's drama and theatre
students. It has also been foremost in promoting
experimental drama in the city, co-operating
with other art/theatre/community organisations,
and generally developing a public interest in
new forms of performance.

The Granary Theatre is a novel and exciting
part of the town-gown relationship.

Drombeg Stone Circle

This spectacular photograph of Drombeg stone circle at sunset on the winter solstice shows UCC archaeologists taking readings towards the 'recumbent' stone. The mysterious ambience of the ancient monument is strikingly evoked and we are also reminded of the continuing association of the college's archaeology department with west Cork excavations and investigations.

Different kinds of stone circles are found in Ireland but, in the Cork and Kerry region (where over 100 are recorded), the characteristic form is the recumbent, or axial, circle. A ring of free-standing stones of varying number and height has an entrance between two matching portal stones, generally the tallest in the circle (in front of the observer in the foreground in this picture). A recumbent, or axial, stone, usually the lowest in the group and placed on its side (in front of the observer in the background), faces the entrance. The main axis from the entrance to the recumbent stone lies northeast to southwest, an orientation that indicates an alignment towards the rising or setting sun.

Perhaps the most impressive ritual monument in west Cork – certainly the best known and one of the best preserved – is the Drombeg stone circle. Drombeg (*drom beag*, a little ridge) is situated about 2 miles east of Glandore. The circle sits on a natural terrace in a commanding position overlooking a cultivated bowl-shaped valley, beyond which the Atlantic is clearly visible. It originally consisted of 17 stones forming an almost perfect circle 9.3 metres in diameter. It was described by its excavator, UCC geographer and archaeologist Edward M. Fahy, as a 'monument of great precision'. A pit in the centre of the circle contained cremated remains and it appears that the site was not used again for this purpose. A *fulacht fiadh*, or burnt mound, is situated 40 metres from the circle itself. Radiocarbon dating indicates that the monument was erected in the Late Bronze Age, between 1200–900 BC.

Drombeg has long been seen as a classic case of winter solstice orientation, but more recent thinking suggests a relationship with lunar movements. At any rate, the circle is 'astronomically determined', as the phrase goes. While professional archaeologists are understandably reluctant to speculate about the purpose and uses of 'sacred' sites and mysterious monuments like Drombeg, lay antiquarians have never had any such inhibitions, and they talk excitedly about ritual burials, sun worship and fertility cults.

Certainly, the stone circle was of major significance in the lives of those who erected it and of their descendants. Today, its scenic location and its magical atmosphere continue to make it an object of never-failing fascination to amateur antiquarians and curious tourists alike. (*For further reading see page 120*)

Geology

The 'List of Accommodation', sent by the
Board of Works in 1846 to the architect of
Queen's College Cork, Sir Thomas Deane,
specified relatively few disciplines for which
space was to be provided but they included
Geology, Natural History and Chemistry.
Robert Harkness, the second professor
(1853–1878) of Mineralogy and Geology at
the college, had an international reputation
and is commemorated by a stained-glass
window in the Aula Maxima. After Harkness,
Geology had a somewhat intermittent
existence in the college but was reinstituted
as a full professorship in 1979.

Natural History

From the beginning of the Queen's College
in 1849 down to the middle of the following
century, there was a large Museum of Natural
History in the North Wing, dominated by a
great Irish 'elk'. There was considerable public
interest in natural history in nineteenth-
century Cork and there has been an unbroken
sequence in the professorship marked only
by a name-change to 'zoology' in the transition
to UCC/NUI in 1908–1909. Throughout
its history, the chair has been held by some
distinguished zoologists. The Zoology
Museum houses many scientifically
important exhibits.

Chemistry

Chemistry was one of the foundation subjects for which separate accommodation was specified (see Geology, p. 102). The first two presidents of the college – Sir Robert Kane (1849–1873) and William Kirby Sullivan (1873–1890) – were both chemists. The subject may not be as popular and glamorous as it once was, but there is no gainsaying its central importance in the development of the biomedical sciences and so much more besides. It is as relevant to industrial research as it was in the time of Kane, whose *Industrial Resources of Ireland* (1844) was of immense importance in Irish industrial history and in the context of economic nationalism.

'Open wide, please' –
Students at the Cork Dental Hospital

The beginnings of the Cork Dental School go back to Sir Bertram Windle's presidency (1904–1919) but it was not put on a university faculty footing until the mid-twentieth century and its future remained problematic for some time thereafter. This was partly a question of external recognition but, more importantly, a matter of financing expensive professional training. If the State needed only a limited number of dental graduates, was a dental school in Cork really necessary? In the end, what carried the day was the crucial and convincing argument that a dental school located in Cork was a necessary community health service for the area.

Vivat academia, vivant professores!

The conferring of honorary degrees is a
grand day on which the sun invariably shines.
Those invited to accept degrees *honoris causa*
(generally, doctorates of science, literature or
law) are introduced in turn in glowing terms
to the invited audience, and are then conferred
by the Chancellor of the University: the former
constituent colleges (Cork, Dublin, Galway
and Maynooth) are now constituent universities
of the National University of Ireland, some-
thing of a mystery in academic theology.
The great and the good are wined and dined.
Those honoured are sometimes well-known
figures drawn from the spheres of sports and
the arts, and they bask for the day in public
adulation spilling far out beyond the groves
of Academe.

Esben Piil Ó Maolcatha

Gaudeamus igitur!

The conferring of degrees on graduation day is a joyous and colourful ceremony, with the pageantry of processions, cap-and-gowns and Latin invocations, following ancient prescribed rituals. (However one young man in this photograph is not impressed by all this solemnity!) Academic staff take time out to acclaim the formal completion of their students' endeavours. Families and friends share the happiness of the occasion while presidents in their conferring addresses air the institution's grievances or make pronouncements on college policy.

In consequence of the setting up of the National University of Ireland, of which Cork was a constituent college, the first conferring ceremony was held on 25 May 1910 in the Aula Maxima, the symbolic heart of the college down all the decades. During the Windle (1904–1919) and Merriman (1919–1943) presidencies, some students treated degree day as an enjoyable indoor rag, an occasion for high jinks, humorous sallies and practical jokes. In 1912, *The Cork Examiner* spoke of 'a wild display of boisterousness', 'uneasiness for the President and the Professors and of pantomimic delight' for the students. The severely sedate President Bertram Windle must have been considerably discomfited by the rhythmic student chant, 'don't hold her hand, Bertie', whenever he conferred a degree on one of the few women graduates. His successor, President P.J. Merriman, would be hailed with a parody ('poor Pad Joe') of a popular 'plantation' song. A railed gallery walkway extending around the Aula facilitated the dropping of stink bombs, flour bags and similar missiles. A picture of the quadrangle on degree day in 1937 looks as if a riot had taken place in the southwestern corner. In 1939, there was an official college complaint that 'hooliganism' had marred the photographing of graduates 'by means of a discharge of sods of grass'.

All these rowdy antics suddenly came to an end when the no-nonsense authoritarian Alfred O'Rahilly became president in 1943 and made it clear that he would no longer indulge these middle-class high spirits. Henceforth, decorum and dignity would prevail and the link between learning and religion underlined, as religious services would precede a sedate procession to the Aula Maxima. This disciplinary clean-up was ensured by packing the Aula with college attendants and by threatening to meet any attempts at disruption with expulsion.

Today, with the ever-increasing proliferation of degree groups, many conferring ceremonies are held in the multi-functional hall of the Students' Building, and the president farms out the speech-giving among distinguished figures in Irish life.

Further Reading

Fahy, Edward M. *A Recumbent Stone Circle at Drombeg, Co. Cork; Journal of the Cork Historical and Archaeological Society*, 64, (1959), 1–27

Fahy, Edward M. *A Hut and Cooking Place at Drombeg, Co. Cork; Journal of the Cork Historical and Archaeological Society*, 65, (1959) 1–17

Leland, Mary (Cork, 2004) *The Honan Chapel: A Guide*

McManus, Damian (Cork, 2004) *Ogham Stones at University College Cork*

Murphy, John A. (Cork, 1995) *The College: A History of Queen's University College Cork, 1845–1995*

Murphy, John A. (Cork, 2006) *University College Cork: A Short History*

O'Dwyer, Frederick (Cork, 1997) *The Architecture of Dean and Woodward*

Ruggles, Clive (Yale 1999) *Astronomy in Prehistoric Britain and Ireland*

Teehan, Virginia and Wincott Hechett, Elizabeth (Cork, 2004) *The Honan Chapel: A Golden Vision*

Waddell, John (Galway 1998) *The Prehistoric Archaeology of Ireland*